Running Effective Marketing Meetings

A how-to guide to run marketing meetings that teach, inspire, and change how you and your team work

Daniel Kuperman

Impackt Publishing
We Mean Business

Running Effective Marketing Meetings

First published: September 2014

Production reference: 1230914

Published by Impackt Publishing Ltd.
Livery Place
35 Livery Street
Birmingham B3 2PB, UK.

ISBN 978-1-78300-018-0

www.impacktpub.com

Cover image by Jarek Blaminsky (milak6@wp.pl)

Credits

Author

Daniel Kuperman

Content Development Editor

Sweny M. Sukumaran

Proofreaders

Simran Bhogal

Ameesha Green

Paul Hindle

Reviewer

Kristi Casey Sanders

Copy Editors

Tanvi Bhatt

Ameesha Green

Production Coordinator

Melwyn D'sa

Acquisition Editor

Nick Falkowski

Project Coordinator

Venitha Cutinho

Cover Work

Melwyn D'sa

About the Author

Daniel Kuperman has over 10 years of marketing, product marketing, and marketing management experience in addition to many years of experience as a management consultant for Fortune 500 clients. He has worked with companies of all sizes including several startups in helping them plan and execute marketing campaigns and programs. As a passionate marketer, he has presented at conferences, written articles, and regularly posts on his blog at www. effectivemarketer.com. Daniel currently leads product marketing for Axcient, a cloud-based provider of disaster recovery and business continuity services. He lives in Mountain View, CA, with his wife and two children. Follow him on Twitter at @danielkuperman.

About the Reviewer

Kristi Casey Sanders is the VP of creative/chief storyteller of Plan Your Meetings. In addition to being an award-winning journalist who has covered meeting industry trends and destinations since 2003, she is a popular speaker on the topics of technology, sustainability, community building, engagement, and proving ROI. Prior to joining the PYM team, she was a corporate trainer/performer with Boom Chicago Comedy Theatre in Amsterdam, where she taught multinational groups soft skills. In her spare time, she is site selection chair for the Society of American Travel Writers' Eastern Chapter, a big-time geek, and a loving mom and wife, not necessarily in that order. Follow her on Twitter at @PYMLive. For more meeting/event planning advice, visit PlanYourMeetings.com or watch her educational broadcasts at YouTube.com/PlanYourMeetings.

In addition to business journalism, she covers Atlanta's art scene with Encore Atlanta. In this capacity, she authored *The Fox Theatre, Atlanta, Georgia: The Memory Maker*, *Atlanta Metropolitan*, an illustrated history of The Fox Theatre's first 80 years.

Contents

Chapter 3: Making Your Meetings Fun   17

Chapter 4: Effectively Conducting Your Meeting   23

Preface

Throughout my marketing career, I have participated in more meetings than I can remember. Those are precious minutes and hours I will never get back. Although some were very productive meetings, the majority were not. It seems it is not a matter of big company versus small company as I have witnessed dysfunctional meetings at companies of all sizes and with different ranks participating.

However, there were a few that stood out as effective meetings where the team felt that something had been accomplished. Some meetings had everyone excited about a certain topic while others were short but very useful. Some meeting organizers really knew how to get people to participate and others had a certain way of making everyone laugh.

It is based on this experience of observing what worked and what didn't, as well as running my own meetings, that I bring you a compilation of what I have seen that really works when it comes to conducting effective marketing meetings.

You don't have to read this book in sequence but if you are new to organizing marketing meetings, it will certainly help.

What this book covers

Chapter 1, Identifying the Meeting Type, covers the most common marketing meetings you will encounter. Not all marketing meetings are the same, and being able to think about the type of meeting you are organizing or that you are attending will help you get better prepared and make it more effective.

Chapter 2, Preparing for the Meeting, is all about how to plan and prepare for an upcoming marketing meeting. We explore some key steps in how to prepare for each type of marketing meeting including the creation of agendas, tools to use, and more.

Chapter 3, Making Your Meetings Fun, is my favorite chapter as we talk about tips and techniques to get attendee participation, different ways to open your meetings, suggestions of other places where you can have your meetings, and how to get people engaged and interested in the topic at hand.

Chapter 4, Effectively Conducting Your Meeting, is where the rubber meets the road, so to speak, because it is all about execution. No amount of planning or preparation can save you from a poorly conducted meeting. Knowing how to properly conduct a meeting is an essential part of having an effective meeting and giving you an opportunity to shine. Here we cover different ways to open the meeting, as well as discussing the importance of an agenda, eliciting participation, closing the meeting, and different tools to help you during the meeting.

Chapter 5, An Effective Meeting Follow up, is often a neglected aspect of running meetings because it deals with what you should do after the meeting is over. Effective meetings require great follow up, so we talk here about writing meeting minutes, taking notes, some different software tools that you can use to help with action items, and how and when to follow up after the meeting.

Chapter 6, Putting Ideas into Practice, is where we wrap up the lessons by adding extra "sauce" to the effective meetings equation. This is where we talk about what makes effective meeting leaders, and we cover being proactive, inquisitive, resourceful, smart, and persistent. With these five concepts, you can take your knowledge about effective meetings and apply it to other areas of the business.

Who this book is for

This book was written for the novice marketer or the recently-promoted marketing manager as a guide to help get the most out of the many meetings they will have to run for the department. Experienced marketing professionals or marketing consultants will also find some new ideas and techniques that they can apply immediately.

Even if they are not in the marketing field, some of the tips and best practices discussed can be transferred over to other functional areas.

Conventions

In this book, you will find a number of styles of text that distinguish between different kinds of information. Here are some examples of these styles, and an explanation of their meaning.

New terms and **important words** are shown in bold.

Make a note
Warnings or important notes appear in a box like this.

Tip
Tips and tricks appear like this.

Reader feedback

Feedback from our readers is always welcome. Let us know what you think about this book—what you liked or may have disliked. Reader feedback is important for us to develop titles that you really get the most out of.

To send us general feedback, simply send an e-mail to feedback@impacktpub.com, and mention the book title via the subject of your message.

If there is a book that you need and would like to see us publish, please send us a note via the **Submit Idea** form on https://www.impacktpub.com/#!/bookidea.

Piracy

Piracy of copyright material on the Internet is an ongoing problem across all media. At Packt, we take the protection of our copyright and licenses very seriously. If you come across any illegal copies of our works, in any form, on the Internet, please provide us with the location address or website name immediately so that we can pursue a remedy.

Please contact us at copyright@impacktpub.com with a link to the suspected pirated material.

We appreciate your help in protecting our authors, and our ability to bring you valuable content.

> 1

Identifying the Meeting Type

Understanding the different types of meetings and when to use each one is the first basic step to running the meeting effectively. The following sections explore the typical meeting types you will encounter in a marketing organization. Note that most of these meetings, if not all, are not exclusive to the marketing department, but I point out some specifics when running these types of meetings with a marketing team in mind.

A staff meeting

They go by many names, but staff meetings are basically the ones where you get together with your team to get status updates, make announcements, and follow up on pending items. In some companies, they are called the **all hands meeting**, others just use **marketing team weekly**, or simply **staff meeting** as the name.

A status report meeting

Sometimes, you will have meetings for the sole purpose of reporting the status of a project, campaign, or other activity. Status report meetings can take many forms, but effective ones are short and to the point. In many situations, a formal face-to-face meeting may not even be required. Many organizations ask that the current status be simply emailed on a weekly basis, unless there are issues that have to be discussed or resolved in person. For larger projects or those that involve cross-departmental teams, it is typical to have face-to-face status report meetings that also provide a way for additional interaction and ensure that all team members are aware of the multiple ongoing activities within the project.

Planning the meeting

Fail to plan and you plan to fail, is how the saying goes. For marketing, nothing is more critical than properly planning your marketing campaigns and projects. Marketing planning meetings typically revolve around annual, quarterly, and monthly planning cycles. Each company is different when it comes to how often and how detailed their marketing plans are, but odds are you will be running a few planning meetings throughout the year. The main goals of these meetings are the setting of targets and metrics, and the overall delineation of what types of marketing activities will be carried out. In some cases, a formal plan of attack is created, and depending on the type of plan you are putting together, input from other departments may be required.

A decision-making meeting

Although a good meeting is sometimes described as a meeting where decisions were made, sometimes you will need to schedule some time to get everyone together to make a final decision on something. It could be a decision on which vendor to select for the next advertising campaign, which software will be implemented for marketing automation, or even which trade shows to attend.

Work meetings

If there is a department that seems to be constantly meeting, marketing is probably on the top of the list. Due to the creative nature of many marketing projects, the marketing team typically meets many times per week (or even per day) to work on one project or another. These meetings are sometimes unstructured conversations among team members, but in other cases these meetings can be formalized and efforts can be coordinated to get something done. An example might be brainstorming new ideas for a promotion, reviewing and commenting on a new website section, or even discussing and editing a video script that showcases a new product.

Evaluation and review meeting

Sometimes bundled together with status report meetings, these types of meetings are typical of any marketing department. After, or even during, the execution of each marketing campaign, you will want to learn what went right and what could be improved. A report of the results is most likely the starting point of this meeting, and a full evaluation will take place so that you can make the necessary course adjustments to the marketing plan and future campaigns.

A report meeting

Depending on the business, marketing is required to provide monthly, quarterly, and annual reports. In many cases, the head of marketing presents a summary of the key marketing metrics, their results, and plans going forward to the senior executive team. In some cases, these meetings are of the closed door type, but in many organizations that pride themselves for transparency, the marketing VP will be asked to deliver the presentation in front of all employees as part of a routine **state of the union** address.

A sales meeting

The coordination of sales and marketing activities is not only critical for the success of a company, but is also of the utmost importance to any top marketing professional. If in your organization marketing doesn't participate in sales meetings, you should address this. Although in most of these meetings, the marketing participation is listen-only, it is a great opportunity to communicate to the sales team the latest campaigns, results, and what is coming down the pipeline of marketing projects.

An offsite meeting

When you hear offsite meeting, you may think of executive offsite where senior managers mingle and discuss the vision for the company and the year ahead. In marketing, you may sometimes want to take the team offsite in order to focus on solving a specific challenge without office distractions, to thoroughly review and reassess important campaigns, and even to stimulate creativity and help with brainstorming new ideas. Properly planning this type of meeting involves careful attention to detail and ensuring the time spent outside the office is well worth it.

A contractor meeting

Marketers use a variety of vendors or contractors to help out with design, copyrighting, trade show management, and more. Whether you have a one-off project with a vendor (for example, a company creating a new video or website for the company) or an ongoing relationship (for example, marketing agency), your meetings with them will set the tone for the relationship. Plan and execute them effectively and you will save both your team's and the contractor's time.

An agile meeting

Borrowed from the **Agile movement** in software development, marketing teams have also been implementing agile techniques in order to gain speed and better results from marketing campaigns. A traditional element of an agile team are their meetings, sometimes called standups. Marketing teams who want to use agile methods will have to adapt to this fast-paced rhythm and different meeting style where the whole team meets for a few minutes every day and focuses on briefly discussing the tasks at hand.

Other meeting types

This is not an exhaustive list of all types of marketing meetings, but this list should cover the most common ones you will encounter. In fact, any time a group of people get together to discuss a common subject, this can be considered a meeting, even if not formally arranged. The important thing to keep in mind is that although meeting types vary, they will all require some basic tools to be effective, which we will cover in the next chapter.

Online meetings

You may be asking yourself why I left online meetings out of the list. Yes, it was on purpose. Although marketing meetings using online conferencing tools such as **WebEx**, **GoToMeeting,** and others, the type of meeting doesn't change, only the way people communicate. The same is true for meetings involving phones and video conferencing. Each tool may need a few adjustments and if you have remote people participating, the leader of the meeting will have to take that into account and plan accordingly. But in the end, they are just tools that can be used to enhance the meeting experience. We will talk more about meeting tools as we address each component of an effective meeting in subsequent chapters.

Meeting goals

Why is it important to understand the different meeting types? Because each one has its own goal or goals. And while at your company they may differ, typically the meeting types I just described will aim for the following:

Meeting type	Typical participants	Goal
Staff meeting	All marketing team	Get the team in sync about the status of various marketing activities, discuss priorities, and plan for the week ahead.
Status report meeting	Marketing manager or director and direct reports	Report on the status of a specific project, campaign, or task. Discuss roadblocks and provide updates on pending issues.
Planning meeting	Marketing leadership and marketing managers	Create marketing action plan for upcoming month/quarter/year.
Decision-making meeting	Marketing leader, marketing manager or campaign owner, and specific team members	Decide on a course of action. Could be related to a project, campaign, vendor, and so on.
Work meeting	Marketing team members	Collaborative work on a specific marketing project.
Evaluation and review	Marketing team or specific campaign members	Assess results of specific campaign or project, extract lessons learned, make necessary course corrections to the marketing plan.
Report meeting	Marketing leaders	Provide management, or other departments with the state of marketing, typically showing plan versus actual.
Sales meeting	Marketing leaders and specific team members when needed	Gain feedback from the sales team, announce campaigns, give relevant updates, and strengthen relationship with sales.
Offsite meeting	Marketing leadership or whole marketing team	Collaborate, brainstorm, or get meaningful work done outside the office.
Contractor meeting	Team member and specific contractor	Introduce, update, or otherwise continue relationship with contractor or vendor.
Agile meeting	Marketing team	Daily standup to provide report on what was done yesterday, what will be done today, and what obstacles stand in the way.

Understanding what you will want to get out of the meeting is the first step to being able to properly plan, execute, and follow-up on a meeting. If you are only a participant and not the organizer or leader of the meeting, then knowing what is expected of the meeting (why are we having this meeting?) will help you get prepared. Not all meeting organizers (as you probably have already experienced) are good meeting organizers. If you can become a better participant, then you can help the meeting be more effective, and then everyone wins.

Summary

In this chapter, we learned that not all marketing meetings are the same. Although they may involve similar elements, and even the same people, they each have different goals and characteristics. By knowing that, you will be able to adequately prepare for each meeting in order to make them successful.

How to prepare and why you should prepare are the next steps and will be covered in the following chapter, so read on and start your journey into the world of effective marketing meetings.

>2

Preparing for the Meeting

"Give me six hours to chop down a tree and I will spend the first four sharpening the axe."

– Abraham Lincoln

Planning versus preparation

There are many ways to prepare for a meeting, and this doesn't have to be a complicated or lengthy process, but if you run a meeting without some basic work up front, it is likely that it will not go well.

I like to think of the pre-meeting (that is, what happens before the meeting) in two separate terms: planning and preparation.

Before scheduling a meeting, define the following:

➤ What is the goal of the meeting?

➤ Who should attend?

➤ How long should the meeting last?

➤ Where should it be held?

➤ What tools or equipment are required?

➤ What advance preparation is required?

If you can answer these questions, your meeting will be off to a good start. You will notice the last point is about what preparation is required, and here is where preparation differs from planning. While planning the meeting is putting together the structure of the meeting itself, preparation is the work you have to do in order to get everything ready for the meeting. This work is sometimes performed by the person organizing the meeting but can also be homework for those attending the meeting. The following examples will help illustrate the different preparation steps required for different types of meetings.

A status report meeting

Preparation for status report meetings may involve sending the status of the project or campaign in question to the meeting attendees, along with notes, pending issues, and other factors. If your goal for the meeting is simply to serve as a means of notification, then by sending all the information beforehand you can help to shorten the meeting duration. If you are lucky, the meeting may not even have to take place!

You may have two preparation activities as well. One would be for the owner of the project or campaign to prepare the report in advance of the meeting and make it available. The other would be to ask all meeting attendees to read the report before coming to the meeting.

Preparation for this type of meeting might also require that pending issues be followed up on, so that an accurate status can be given during the meeting. Depending on the type of project and who is attending, you may have to brief certain individuals in advance (for example, you may know that there is an issue with the project that requires a certain VP to take action, so you may want to give this VP a heads up so that he or she can come to the meeting prepared to tackle the issue, and therefore save time).

Tip

Be prepared to report on the status of your campaigns and projects. Include information such as: name of campaign/project, planned results, actual results, issues or obstacles, and notes.

Planning the meeting

Preparation for a marketing planning meeting can take many forms. You may want to give your team some materials to read before the meeting, you may want the team to send you ideas prior to the meeting date, or you may want to have something special arranged in advance (such as a video, a case study, or consolidated reports from previous years).

Tip

Come prepared for planning meetings with information about previous campaign results, monthly and quarterly goals, and other relevant metrics that will help put together a solid plan.

A decision-making meeting

In this kind of meeting, the preparation is typically done by laying out the problem at hand and all the facts available. For example, if you have to ask your boss to approve your budget, you want to make sure you are prepared with not only the proposed budget, but also with information on what your budget was in previous years, why each budget item is necessary, and so on.

If you are the one that has to make a decision, then look at all the past historical data available to you. Let's say you were asked to make a decision on which marketing agency to choose. Before meeting with your team to talk about it and announce your decision, make sure you have reviewed the proposals, the work samples submitted, and other input you may have from your team.

Tip

When looking at multiple options, also take into consideration the cost of doing nothing. Sometimes it can be a compelling factor.

Work meetings

People seldom do much preparation when they know they have to go to a work meeting or working session. We are going to be working during that meeting on this same topic, so why prepare in advance? Well, depending on the type of work you need the team to do, you can ask them to prepare by jotting down ideas, reading materials, or even doing preliminary work.

For example, let's say you schedule a work meeting so that the team can discuss and come up with a new navigation structure for the company's website. Prior to the meeting taking place, you may want everyone to review the website individually and make notes. You may want your web designer to send everyone the latest report from Google Analytics showing the top pages visited and top exit pages. You may also want the product marketing manager to send everyone links to competitors' websites. The list goes on.

Tip

For effective working sessions, make sure everyone is committed to the task at hand by blocking off that time in their calendars and telling their colleagues not to be disturbed. Also turn off laptops or resist checking e-mails during the meeting.

An evaluation and review meeting

Preparing for an effective evaluation and review meeting requires the data that the evaluation will be based on to be sent in advance. If campaign results will be discussed, sending them in advance to team members will give everyone a chance to look at the data and come prepared with questions. If different people are responsible for different elements of a campaign that will be reviewed, then asking each member to bring specific reports for their areas (and send them in advance if possible) can also make the meeting more effective.

Tip

Be proactive and don't just recite the results of your campaign, but rather bring ideas of how to improve and what lessons you learned from the results.

A report meeting

Preparation of your actual report is obvious, but what may not be so obvious is the context or the detailed data behind it. If you are preparing to give a monthly or quarterly report to the executive team of your company, be ready for questions that require you to drill down in to more detailed data. Whether by having a separate handout, an extra PowerPoint file on your laptop, or slide notes, you will be thankful that you are well-prepared.

Tip

Want your report to be read? Less is more. Focus only on the key indicators and the most important information. Use visuals if they will help tell the story.

A sales meeting

If you are only participating in, and not organizing a sales meeting (or meeting with any other department), then your best way to prepare is to read the agenda beforehand and get acquainted with the topic. Ideally you will want to ask the sales manager or the person running that meeting what kind of participation they would like from you and what you should expect from the meeting. You don't want to be caught off-guard when they ask you about results of a campaign you are not prepared to talk about.

Tip

Be proactive and approach the sales leadership team with ideas of what to share during their meetings. Better sales and marketing collaboration and communication is good for everyone.

An offsite meeting

Offsite meetings require a lot of preparation time because you need to choose the right location, map out the travel logistics, rent AV equipment, think about menus and a million other moving parts. When you're that busy with minutia, it's easy to loose sight of the big picture. But nothing's more frustrating than feeling like getting everyone out of the office was waste of time. To ensure that everyone feels like going offsite was effective, make sure you think about:

> ➤ How can we use this space (out of the office) to our advantage?
>
> ➤ What team dynamics can be explored in this space?
>
> ➤ How can we keep people's attention and focus?
>
> ➤ What should we ask them to bring and what do we want them to take back?

Tip

Don't think an offsite meeting has to involve fancy hotels or other locations. The other building your team never uses, a different conference room, and even a restaurant can be good offsite locations. The goal is to take the team out of their typical surroundings.

A contractor meeting

Meetings with contractors are typically straightforward but if not prepared well, they can be time-consuming. For meetings to go smoothly, make sure you check on the latest communications you had with them, review their deliverables, and send any preparation details you want them to take in advance.

For example, if a meeting with a freelance graphic designer will be about a new billboard idea you have, make sure you send the specifications of that billboard in advance, as well as any previous billboards your company has used, and ask the graphic designer to come ready to discuss new ideas as well as the stated agenda items.

Tip

Bring your scope of work and any pertinent technical details to the meeting and, if possible, email them in advance to the contractor.

An agile meeting

Agile meetings usually comprise daily standup meetings where the team spends 15 minutes discussing what they accomplished last week, what their priorities are for this week, and what is in their pipeline for the following week. Preparing for these types of meetings require everyone to get their action item updated and ready to be discussed.

Tip

Fight the urge to share everything and talk about every project. Focus on the most important tasks at hand, the upcoming deadlines, and any obstacles in your path.

Effective preparation

What is an effective meeting? Chad Harrington, VP of Marketing at Adaptive Computing suggests an effective meeting is defined as follows:

> *"An effective meeting is a meeting that met its stated objectives..."*

Chad is right. You can spend all the time in the world making preparations, but if at the end of the meeting you didn't accomplish your goals or objectives, then the meeting was a waste of everyone's time.

The first step to ensuring that your meeting will be successful (that is, it will meet its objectives) is to think about how you and your team can be prepared so that the meeting time is used efficiently and the meeting goals are met.

Summary

In this chapter, we covered how to prepare for the different types of marketing meetings you are likely to encounter at most organizations. While good meetings require proper planning, preparation is where most people fall short. With the tips in this chapter, you are now able to get take the right steps to ensure your meetings are effective. While focusing on preparation is good, we also want to give you some tools that will help you run your meetings successfully. Continue to the next chapter for some best practices on conducting effective meetings.

3

Making Your Meetings Fun

Who says meetings can't be fun? Think about it, why spend time in a room with other people instead of actually doing your work? If meetings are inevitable, you might as well find ways to make them more interesting, which in turn will help you achieve the meeting's goals.

Common pitfalls

You probably have and will experience many poorly planned meetings that seem to suck the life out of everyone in the room. To avoid the same mistakes others have made, first you must be aware of them. The following is a list of common meeting pitfalls:

- ➤ **No clear agenda**: This leads to unprepared attendees and no clear goal to accomplish, which makes attendees feel like the meeting was a waste of time. Make sure everyone knows the agenda and the goal for the meeting. Best practice is to print the agenda, have it shown on a screen, or write it on a whiteboard for everyone to see at the start of the meeting.

- ➤ **Delayed start**: This is not only disrespectful to the attendees, but also forces the meeting to either go beyond the allotted time or rush the discussion. Make it a matter of habit to start your meetings promptly, even if you need to arrive a few minutes earlier to set up, it will be worth it. As people realize you start every meeting on time, they will start making it on time.

- ➤ **Going off-topic**: This could lead to time wasted discussing something other than the reason the meeting was scheduled. When you see a discussion starts bordering on another topic that is not in the agenda, kindly pause the discussion and suggest it be either taken off-line or mark it as a good subject for another meeting.

Tip

A **parking lot** is typically used to take note of items that do not belong to the meeting at hand and you can have it on a whiteboard or a flipchart so everyone can see the items that will be covered in a separate meeting.

> ➤ **The meeting is hijacked by another participant**: This makes you lose the opportunity to take care of items listed in the agenda. Avoid this by making sure everyone agrees with the agenda and has no items to add as the first thing you do when you start a meeting. If another participant still takes the discussion off-topic, use the parking lot technique, or ask the attendees whether they think the topic should be discussed. If they do, declare the meeting adjourned and to be rescheduled so that the issue can be resolved.

> ➤ **The meeting runs over the allotted time**: This may reflect poorly on the organizer and force people to leave without having accomplished the goals for the meeting. By starting on time, you reduce the chances of this happening. Another technique is to identify the allotted time for each topic in the agenda (which is done by asking the topic's owner how much time they think will be required). At the end of each topic's timeframe, announce that the time is over. It may seem weird at first, but everyone will thank you for keeping the meeting going and respecting everyone's time.

> ➤ **Not being prepared or not asking people to prepare beforehand**: This can lead to wasted time, poor meeting execution, and confusion about the reason for the meeting. You obviously fix this by making sure you are prepared and by taking the appropriate steps before the meeting such as distributing any reading materials and even sending an e-mail reminder the day before the meeting.

> ➤ **Key people absent from the meeting**: This means decisions might be delayed, the meeting may be seen as wasted time, and another meeting will have to be scheduled with the missing participants. There are two ways to handle this, the first being to make sure that key people are aware of the meeting before the meeting and have confirmed their presence, and the second being that you may want to postpone the meeting if key people are not present at the start of it. It is better to reschedule a meeting rather than to have all that time wasted by not being able to make decisions.

Rethinking the approach to meetings

Should meetings always be held in a conference room or someone's office? One way to get more out of meetings and make them effective is to rethink how you prepare for and conduct your meetings. The following sections contain some ideas that might help get more out of your marketing meetings.

Invite another department

Talking about the results of a campaign? Ask the CFO to join for a few minutes and share the costs associated with the campaign with the team, or ask the sales manager to join to give his view of the leads that were generated and what feedback the sales team has.

Make it a standing-only meeting

Instead of sitting down, make everyone stand up during the meeting. People are less likely to divert their attention from the topic at hand while standing and it makes for a more dynamic discussion. Agile marketing standup-meetings are named this way because everyone is supposed to be standing up while talking about what they've done and what they will accomplish during the week.

Go outside the office

If it's a nice day outside, go out of the building. Take a walk to the nearest coffee shop or if your company has lawn chairs on a patio you can use, take advantage of it. A change of scenery is a great way to get people energized.

Walk and talk

Not very practical for large groups, but for one-on-one meetings or up to three people, you could take a walk while discussing things.

Eat while meeting

Try changing the dynamics a bit by either meeting for breakfast or having a lunch meeting. Instead of the typical catered lunch where you are still in the office, go to a restaurant and ask either for a private room or a quiet table in the corner so your team can talk with more privacy.

Use a whiteboard

Ditch the PowerPoint slides and use a whiteboard or flipchart instead. When you go to a whiteboard and start drawing or writing, you capture people's attention more easily than by projecting something on the screen. If your meeting is being conducted with remote employees, use an online meeting tool that has a whiteboard capability or just open a blank document and share your screen while you type. Post-it notes are also a great way to get people to focus and share ideas as you write things down and place them along the wall.

Don't treat it as a meeting

According to Mike Volpe, CMO for HubSpot, meetings should sometimes be thought of as performances, as if you were presenting to a group:

> *"People think of meetings as "meetings" rather than performances or conversations. A meeting should be one of those things, but not both. Any meeting with more than 10-15 people needs to be viewed not as a meeting but as a performance. The presenter is onstage and should think of it like a keynote presentation where you have to command the attention of the audience by performing. Don't read the text on the slides, be prepared, have some jokes or stories. On the other hand, any meeting with fewer people should also be engaging, but the engagement should be based on communication and collaboration. Ask questions, get feedback, make it a discussion to get people involved."*
>
> *– Mike Volpe, CMO, HubSpot*

Marketing meetings as educational opportunities

Fun meetings are those you typically don't forget, or at least you don't regret having attended. Fun doesn't have to mean getting your team to have good laughs but rather a good time. One way of doing this and having meetings that people actually don't mind attending, is to make it educational. Make sure you don't make the meeting similar to a class at school, but if in every meeting that you host, the attendees actually learn something interesting, they will be more likely to pay attention and will want to attend your meetings. Some ideas are given in the following sections.

Start with a fact

At the beginning of the meeting, share some interesting fact about the company, a recent marketing campaign, or even an industry insight with the team. If the fact (could be a statistic, a quote, numerical results, charts, and so on) is connected to the meeting topic, the better it is.

Word of the day

This is something the CEO at one of the companies I worked for used to do. It started off as a joke at an executive meeting but became something people looked forward to in every meeting he hosted. He would start with "So, today's word is…" and he would say a word that was not typically used colloquially and ask people to say out loud what they thought the meaning or a synonym was. Not only did it make the start of meetings interesting and act as a kind of icebreaker, it also increased everyone's vocabulary.

Talk about an interesting article

As part of your meeting preparation, you can either send people a link to an interesting marketing article you found or you can share it with them during the meeting. Highlight why the article is relevant to the meeting (make it a point to include it in the agenda) and people will read it beforehand. You can also bring it up to help you make a point during the meeting by citing the article or sharing a summary about it with the team at an appropriate point in the meeting.

Share the knowledge

Make a habit of asking one team member to share something interesting he or she has learned recently at the beginning of every meeting. This forces people to keep current with industry trends and keep learning. If at the start of each meeting, you randomly select who will be sharing that day, everyone will want to be prepared in case they are called on to be the person to share their story or learning.

Choose a leader

Instead of being the one who runs the meetings, ask someone else in the team to do it. Sure, you will want to have this person prepared, so don't do it on-the-spot, but rather ask the person as early as possible. This is perfect to train team members on how to run meetings, take more responsibility, and get them excited.

Use questions instead of topics

Instead of having a discussion around a topic, create an agenda that has questions that need to be answered. For example, if the meeting is to review results of a recent campaign, phrase the agenda items as questions such as "Why are our conversion rates declining? " instead of "Review conversion rates for ABC campaign." Instead of using "E-mail metrics from the latest campaign", use "What can we do to improve e-mail click through rates from 10 percent to 25 percent?", and this way, participants have to actively think about the possible answers. At the very least, they will have to come prepared with ideas for the meeting, which could make it more productive and even more interesting.

Summary

In this chapter, we learned that meetings don't have to be serious or boring affairs. In fact, changing the way your marketing meetings are conducted by inserting some fun activities and rethinking your approach to meetings in general can yield better results. We looked at the common pitfalls to avoid and also at some tools that can transform your meetings into educational opportunities. All of this, however, is dependent upon on how properly you conduct or execute your marketing meetings, which is what we will cover in the next chapter.

> 4

Effectively Conducting Your Meeting

Proper planning and preparation are essential for conducting an effective meeting, but will be of no help unless you also know how to run the meeting. In this chapter, we take a look at some techniques you can use to make sure your meetings run smoothly and give you tips on how to handle the most common situations you will encounter.

Opening the meeting

You can tell a meeting will be effective right from the start because of the way it is opened. Is there a clear agenda? Are participants introduced? Are goals explained? Following are some key things to consider when opening your meeting.

Roll call

Is everyone present or do you need to wait a few minutes, or even modify the order of items in the agenda because key participants haven't arrived yet? For meetings in person, this is easily done by looking at who is present, but for those involving remote employees and contractors that are dialing into a conference line or web meeting, you should do a quick roll call to see who is present. Note that if you always start meetings on time, people will learn how important it is to show up promptly.

Introductions

Right after your roll call should be introductions if people who have not met before are attending the meeting. This is especially useful when meeting marketing agencies and contractors (either virtually or physically) so that roles and responsibilities are clearly identified up front.

Agenda

The best way to make sure everyone sticks to the agenda is to go over it at the start of the meeting. Restate the purpose of the meeting and go through the agenda items. Ask whether everyone agrees with the items and whether they have anything else to add to the agenda (provided there will be time to cover those items, of course).

Note-taking

For some meetings you may want to assign someone to take notes, which could be just writing them down on a piece of paper or even using a whiteboard. By having someone take notes, you ensure that major decisions are being recorded and you free yourself from having to stop the discussion because you have to write down what was just discussed. It can also help junior members of the team focus and learn more about the topic being discussed. Paperless note-taking is possible now via mobile apps such as Peak Meetings and TheMeetingApp.com.

Warm up

A good way to get everyone to warm up to the meeting is to start off with something unexpected or an icebreaker. Some ideas were discussed in our previous chapter such as starting with a question, a joke, an interesting fact, or even by giving an award to someone. Even showing a brief movie clip that is related to the topic or that you will use as example for discussion during the meeting could be a good way to start things off.

Ground rules

In some cases, you may want to also talk about some ground rules for the meeting, which is especially useful if it will involve brainstorming, going over a complex project, or when a topic (for example, a new website redesign or new marketing campaign) could easily create some tangential discussions. Ground rules include reminding everyone of the agenda topics, when the meeting will end, any parking lot options, and so on.

For example, you could say "Thank you everyone for attending today's meeting. Before we jump into the discussion I would like to go over why we are here today, have our team introduce themselves and in turn our marketing agency group to also do quick introductions, especially in regards to who handles copywriting, design, and so forth. We are scheduled to end this meeting at 3pm and to make sure we end on time, I want us to stick to the agenda. Any items that come up that we should address in a separate meeting I will write down on this side of the whiteboard. I have asked Jennifer to take notes for us today."

Tips for a strong opening

Each marketing meeting has a different purpose as we saw in *Chapter 1, Identifying the Meeting Type*. We will explore some tips to make sure you open each type of meeting on a strong note in the following sections.

A staff meeting

State the purpose of the meeting and the order in which you would like people to speak. For example, "Thank you everyone for coming to today's marketing staff meeting. It is important that we are all in sync and have an idea what everyone is working on and what is coming down the pipeline. Let's begin counter-clockwise today with John, followed by Mary, and so on. John, tell us what you have."

A status report

Ensure everyone knows which project, campaign, or activity you are giving a status on and any key learning point. It could go something like this: "I am here to give you an update on our back-to-school campaign launched last month. I would like to show you some key highlights of the campaign such as how our click-through rates have been higher than expected, and also share some areas of improvement such as landing page conversion rates which show only 20 percent, while our typical conversion rate is closer to 42 percent."

Planning the meeting

Review the goals for this planning session and clarify how much detail you expect. Do you want the team to discuss high-level campaigns and budget, or to detail specific action items? It is also good to show them how this planning session will influence other areas (marketing budget, quarterly results, and so on) and how it is connected with previous plans.

Decision making

Review the agenda and make sure everyone understands the decision or decisions that need to be made by the end of the meeting. For example, "Before we begin, let me just review our goals for today. We have three decisions to make: the first being whether we will continue using our current agency or look for another one; the second is whether we will kill the back-to-school campaign or give it another month; and finally we need to decide who will be speaking at the next industry event."

Work meeting

Working sessions can easily turn in the wrong direction if not focused on a specific project or topic, so before starting to actually work, review the purpose of the meeting, how long you will be meeting for, and what you expect to get out of it.

A report meeting

I like to use the same tactic as explained with the status report meeting. You are going to report on the state of the marketing department (plan versus actual) so your best bet is to give a quick overview and bring a summary of the good and the bad before you dive into details.

A sales meeting

If you are a participant, it might be good in the beginning to state why you are there. For example: "Hello everyone. I'm Daniel, from the marketing team and I'm just here to listen to your feedback about last week's campaign and take notes on what we can do to improve."

If you are an active speaker with some time allotted during the meeting, talk to the sales manager or the person in charge of the meeting to make sure they tell everyone why you are there (for example, "And today we have Daniel, from the marketing team, who will come up here after we cover our monthly results to talk to you about..."). This avoids people thinking "What is this person doing here?" and avoids distractions.

A offsite meeting

You want to make the most of your and your team's time when out of the office, but at the same time keep a tight schedule. Make sure that you talk about why you are all there, why that particular place was chosen, what the agenda for the day looks like, what you want to get out of it, and also cover the logistics (where are the bathrooms? When will there be breaks? Lunch? and so on).

A contractor meeting

This one is a mixture of the previous tips, since you could have contractors in every type of meeting. It's important when meeting with contractors to set the ground rules and especially to start with the right expectations for what the meeting will accomplish. For example, is the purpose of the meeting to review the scope? Discuss timelines? Approve the project?

An agile meeting

Agile meetings are quick, without much room for anything else other than getting right to business and asking them to tell you what they have completed, what they have on their plate this week, and what is coming up. Start by just making sure everyone is there and set the pace.

Eliciting participation

Want people to actively participate in your meetings? You may have to provoke them a bit. The following are some good ways to get the team involved.

Use props

Bring a tennis ball or some other kind of soft ball and gently throw it at the person you are asking a question, or at the person who just spoke up. Other props like that can make for a dynamic meeting environment and can be fun at the same time.

Call out their names

Instead of using the generic statement "So, who has an idea of what we can do about this?" ask someone by name, like "Ben, do you have any thoughts on this topic?" for example.

Use their areas of expertise

People typically think in terms of their own areas of expertise and responsibility and may not be aware that they can or should provide input unless prompted to do so. You can appeal to their expertise when eliciting their opinion by saying "Mark, help us think this through from a design perspective?" or "Jen, do you have anything to add? Maybe there's something from a lead generation point of view that we should consider?".

Tell them you value their opinions

If there's a person that has not been very participatory, you could ask him or her to contribute to the discussion by saying you value their opinion, like "Gail, you have been very quiet. I would really like to know what you think about this, you always have good insight" or "Bob, you are always keeping us up to date on new technology, so what do you think about…".

Assign a meeting or topic leader

A good way to get people to participate and be prepared for the meeting is to make them the meeting leader or assign them to lead the discussion of a topic. By giving them this responsibility, they will more likely be prepared and ready to participate. If the meeting focuses on a topic that one team member is either very familiar with or has been working on, make that person the meeting leader.

Sticking to the agenda

Get your meeting started on time, end it on time, and stick to the agenda, and you will be surprised at how much more effective it will be. Sure, sticking to the agenda can be tricky sometimes, but the following are some tips on how to make sure the agenda is not forgotten:

> ➤ Create and distribute the agenda a few days before the meeting and ask for everyone's input.

> ➤ Follow up with key participants to make sure they agree with the agenda and don't have any items to add.

> ➤ Assign a specific duration for each item in the agenda. This is a good way to make sure people think about those items and whether there will be enough time, especially if each item is owned by a different person.

> ➤ Get everyone to agree at the beginning of the meeting that the agenda will be followed.

> ➤ Stop any off-topic discussion by assigning a "parking lot" where those ideas will be recorded for later discussion.

> ➤ Keep track of time and do a time-check every once in a while (for example, "I'm sorry to interrupt this discussion, but just want to do a quick time check; we have been talking about point 3 for a while and we still have points 4 and 5 to cover and only 15 minutes left, should we move on?").

Meeting tools

You will run a more effective meeting if you use the appropriate tools, and each meeting may require a different set of tools. If remote employees or contractors are involved, using web conferencing software is a good way to keep everyone on topic as you share your computer screen or even video during the meeting.

Whiteboards and flip charts are great aides to get ideas out and can also help to keep meetings on track. Note-taking software such as **Evernote** can be a good sidekick for you at any meeting since you can not only type in notes that can later be easily distributed, you can also record voice notes. I have also seen people using the **LiveScribe** pen, which looks like a regular pen but digitizes everything you write and can also record voice together with your notes. Laser pointers and remote clickers are good when presenting charts or slides.

And how about food? They are not tools per se, but can be of great help to get people engaged and focused. Serving some coffee and pastries for an early morning meeting is a good way to get people to arrive on time, and having coffee or some cookies in the afternoon can provide a boost in productivity as well. Although, bear in mind that current trends favor brain-friendly foods such as nuts and whole fruit, which refuel people without leaving them feeling weighted down or sleepy like heavy pastries and sugary foods do.

Part of your preparation should be to think about which tools can be more useful during the meeting.

Tip

Sample Meeting Tech Tools

- Evernote, for taking notes and sharing them with the team: www.evernote.com
- Join.me, Webex, GoToMeeting, MeetingBurner, and other conferencing tools to help meet with remote employees: www.join.me, www.webex.com, www.gotomeeting.com, www.meetingburner.com
- MindMeister, MindJet, Xmind, and other mind mapping software can help create an agenda, keep track of notes, and share them with the team: www.mindmeister.com, www.mindjet.com, www.xmind.net
- GoogleDocs, for creating and sharing meeting agendas and minutes for free: docs.google.com
- Todoist, Wunderlist, Producteev, and other task list management software can help you keep track of action items during your meetings and track their completion: www.todoist.com, www.wunderlist.com, www.producteev.com.

Closing the meeting

As you close your meeting, there is one very important question you should ask yourself, and even the participants: were the meeting objectives accomplished? And there is even one more point to consider: what should be done now that the meeting is over?

If no decisions were made during the meeting and no action items were assigned, then why was the meeting scheduled in the first place? Effective meetings also require effective ways of making sure the time wasn't wasted. The following are some suggestions on how to close your meetings:

- **Quickly review** all the decisions that were made either by writing them down on a whiteboard or by calling them out loud.

- **Review all action items** assigned during the meeting, their owners, and deadlines. It might be good if instead of reading them out loud, you ask individual participants to share their specific action items with the team, which ensures they are paying attention and agree with what was assigned to them.

- **Agree on the next steps**, even if there isn't a next step. This could be "Okay, so before we adjourn, our next step will be for Bob to review the website analytics reports, send everyone a copy and schedule a follow-up meeting so we can make a decision on which area of the website will be worked on first," or "Okay, so it seems we have accomplished everything we set out in the agenda. Are we in agreement that everything related to this topic has been resolved and we don't have to meet again about this?"

➤ **Write up** the meeting minutes and distribute them quickly. Don't try to capture and re-create the whole meeting, just focus on key decisions and action items. E-mail everyone no more than one day after the meeting and highlight the important next steps, if any. We will cover more details about meeting minutes in our next chapter.

➤ **Thank everyone for attending**, it sounds simple, but not only is it good form, it also makes everyone feel better when you thank them.

Summary

Running meetings can be challenging, but with a few tips you can get things under control and ensure your goals are achieved. You now have a good checklist for opening your meeting, some tips for a strong opening based on the type of meeting, and two important things to keep in mind at all times: always stick to the agenda and close the meeting properly to end on a high note. We also covered some tips to elicit participation and some handy tech tools you can use to make your meetings more effective. Now that you have plenty of ammunition to use when conducting your next meeting, in the next chapter, we will cover the important but often neglected aspect of following up after a meeting.

> 5

An Effective Meeting Follow up

When the marketing team meets, there is typically a laundry list of things that come out of it. Decisions were made that might impact a current campaign, discussions about a new design could require some rework, and a brainstorming session that generated many new ideas sparked a few interesting new campaign possibilities. Regardless of the meeting, it is likely that the end of the meeting is just the beginning.

So whether you were the organizer or just a participant, properly following up after the meeting is what will actually determine if the meeting was successful in achieving its objectives. Let's explore a few options.

Meeting minutes

The minutes of a meeting (also called meeting notes) refer to the written record of that meeting. The basic idea for the minutes is that you will have recorded the key elements of the meeting, which typically include:

> - Date and time
> - Location
> - Participants
> - Topics discussed
> - Decisions made
> - Action items (Who? What? When?)

The writing of meeting minutes serves three purposes: firstly, it communicates to those who were not able to attend the results of the meeting; secondly, it documents decisions and action items, which meeting participants can refer to after the meeting; and thirdly, it serves as a record for posterity (especially useful if the project is later audited, or new people are assigned to it and have to understand its history).

Good meeting minutes will have the following characteristics:

> **Succinct**: There is no need to capture everything that was said in the meeting, only the key topics and decisions need to be covered.

> **Action-oriented**: It should be action-oriented so that someone reading it can easily identify what actions need to be taken, by whom, and when.

> **Follows the agenda**: Each agenda item is identified and specific decisions or action items related to that item were recorded.

Who writes the minutes? It depends. As the organizer, you can take notes during the meeting and write them yourself, or you can ask (or assign) someone else to do it. As a participant in a meeting, it is good practice for you to take notes unless someone has been clearly identified as the official note-taker. If your company is not following proper meeting practices, then as a participant you can start influencing the team to slowly adopt effective meeting behavior (giving them a copy of this book might be a good starting point!).

So if you are the organizer, you could say "Thank you everyone for attending our meeting today. Before we start, I just want to let you know that I will be taking notes and will send meeting minutes after this meeting to everyone," or "Bob, could you help me and be the official note-taker for today's meeting?".

If you are just a participant, you can volunteer by saying "Just one thing before we begin, I will be taking notes throughout the meeting and jotting down action items. I will later send everyone an e-mail with a summary and what was decided". Volunteering to do something that will benefit the whole team is a good way to earn kudos and be noticed.

Taking notes during a meeting

This is not an end to the subject of meeting minutes, but rather an addendum. Unless you take good notes, you won't be able to generate great minutes, so let's take a closer look at note-taking. It may sound simple, but if you are just starting out in your marketing career, you should develop a good note-taking habit. If you are already up in the marketing management ladder, a quick review of how to take effective notes won't hurt.

Paper or electronic?

Some people prefer using a pen and paper to take notes while others can't leave their laptops or iPads at their desks. The traditional paper method is inconspicuous and shows others that you are paying attention. Unless you run out of ink (or paper), you don't need to worry about not being able to continue taking notes. Also, the habit of manually writing something down on paper helps some people to better remember a conversation. By using shorthand (not writing every word and using abbreviations), writing it by hand can be quite fast.

The advantages of electronic note-taking are obvious. Everything you type can easily and quickly be converted into the meeting minutes with minor edits. Also, software such as **Evernote** is great for keeping notes in order, and mind-mapping tools such as **MindManager**, **MindMeister**, or **Xmind** allow you to take notes in an unstructured way. The drawbacks are that besides the possibility of running low on battery, it could make other participants uneasy by making them question "Is this person really taking notes or checking their e-mail?". I know some marketing teams who have banned the use of laptops during meetings so that people don't get distracted by incoming e-mails, instant messages, and other stuff popping up on their screens while the meeting is in progress.

An example of meeting notes using online mind mapping software **MindMeister** is shown in the following screenshot:

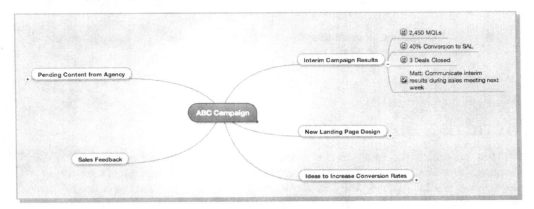

I have also seen people with a combination of both methods, which uses something like a **LiveScribe** pen. This inventive technology gives you what looks like a regular pen that you can write with but it records everything you write and say and can later be plugged into your computer to completely download your notes and audio.

Note-taking tips

Each note-taking method has its own merits and can follow the same tips. The various note-taking tips are discussed in the following sections.

> **Be organized**: During meetings, discussions can go wildly off topic until they are brought back to the agenda and a lot of different opinions are voiced when deciding to make a decision on whether to approve the new layout for a landing page. If you are taking notes, make sure you group all action items together, all pending issues next to each other, and so on. This will not only make for easy note-taking, but will help when creating meeting minutes or looking up what your own actions are.

> **Use shorthand and acronyms**: Write (or type) fast by summarizing things, using abbreviations, and shortening words. You can later rephrase and expand when creating the minutes.

> **Draw, use symbols or illustrations**: Using symbols such as empty squares for action items, exclamation points next to important decisions, and question marks for items to be followed up on are good ways to make your notes easier to read and remember.

> **Use a projector or whiteboard**: If using a laptop, use a projector so that everyone can see your notes as you are taking them. This could help clarify questions, make sure you are capturing important items, and serves as a confirmation that everyone agrees to certain decisions being made. Another great way to take notes and get people's attention is to write on a whiteboard. Get up and as decisions are made or questions raised, write them on the whiteboard. At the end of the meeting, you can snap a picture of the whiteboard with your smartphone to serve as a guide for creating meeting notes. For virtual/online meetings, share your screen as you type in your notes so everyone can see.

> **Use the agenda**: A great template for meeting minutes is the agenda itself. Print out a copy and take notes next to each item.

Follow these tips and you will have effective and actionable notes from your meetings.

Sending out meeting minutes

It is best practice to send out meeting minutes within one business day of the end of the meeting. If you wait too long, you risk people not reading it or your notes becoming outdated. E-mail is typically the best way to do it, especially with remote teams. Whether you type the meeting notes directly into the body of the e-mail or as an attachment will depend on what your notes contain. The benefit of having it all in the e-mail body is that those looking at your e-mail from their mobile devices will easily see the minutes without having to download the file and then find a good way to open the attachment.

Make use of colors and highlighting to point everyone to the important things in your minutes, namely the decisions made and the action items.

When to follow up

Just because everyone agreed during the meeting that certain actions would be taken doesn't mean they will actually do it. Priorities change, holidays approach, and other meetings might get in the way. A gentle follow up is sometimes a good reminder that something needs to be done. Look at the deadlines identified for each action item and check with each owner a few days before to see how things are going.

In some organizations where e-mails rule, a good way to follow up on action items and make sure they are being taken care of is to simply send an e-mail reminder. Something with the subject "FUP on Action Item...." stating in the body of the e-mail that you are simply following up and want a status update might suffice.

In other corporate environments, you may have to personally talk to the action-item's owner for a status update.

Instant messaging, now prevalent in most companies, can also come in handy when following up on action items. Open a new IM window and casually ask about the item that person was responsible for.

However, after you ask people for their status on action items, what do you do with that information?

You will have to do the following:

> ➤ Ask whether the action item was completed
> ➤ If not, ask for a date when it will be completed
> ➤ Ask whether there is anything preventing the person from completing the action item
> ➤ Compile all statuses and report back to the team

This last item is critical. Send everyone that was in the meeting an "Action Items Update" e-mail showing all action items, their owners, and the status. If a new meeting has been scheduled on the same topic, make sure you highlight the day and time of the meeting as a reminder.

Summary

Following up after a meeting is the best way to ensure that the meeting objectives are met. Typically, many action items and decisions will have been made and it might be your job to make sure all that time spent was not in vain. In this chapter, we covered best practices for creating meeting minutes, sending them out, and following up with team members. This is the last step of effective meetings, which started with planning and preparation, followed by execution and closing of the meeting. We covered a lot of information, so next up we will talk a little bit about how to make use of all the material presented in this book.

>6

Putting Ideas into Practice

Now that we have covered all the theory, it is up to you to put it into practice. If you are a marketing manager or higher, this should be easy, but if you are still in the early stages of your marketing career, you will face some challenges. The following sections contain some advice to help you get started.

Five steps to effective marketing meetings

If you know what is best practice when running marketing meetings, you should always strive for the best. Even if you are not the one in charge or if someone else in the team has called the meeting, it is your job and in your best interest to start spreading the word of what effective marketing meetings look like.

Be proactive

Did you receive a meeting invitation without an agenda? Is the team coming to the decision that a meeting will be required to finalize work or make a decision about something? Be proactive and volunteer to help. For example, you could say, "Bob, I think having a meeting to review the new landing pages the agency created is great! If you'd like, I can help create the agenda and prepare for the meeting," or "Mary, I just received this meeting invitation and since it is related to a work I am currently doing, I wouldn't mind helping you prepare the agenda and think about the goals for meeting...".

Be inquisitive

Asking questions is sometimes the best way to get people thinking in other terms. Got a meeting invitation without an agenda? The meeting goals are not clear? Ask. For example, you could say "Matt, what is the goal for the meeting you just invited us for? I want to make sure I am prepared," or "Bill, before we begin, can we quickly go through the goals for the meeting so that we use our time wisely?" or even, "Before we begin, who is taking notes and sending out the meeting minutes?".

Be resourceful

Based on the advice in this book, create what you think would be a good agenda and minutes templates for your own marketing meetings. As you see meetings being scheduled and conducted, start using those templates and offering them to others, for example, "Ann, thanks for taking notes today. Here's a meeting minutes template you could use if you think it's helpful". Start talking to other team members about the things you learned in this book and suggest ideas for the next meeting. Be seen as someone that is willing to share best practices and is interested in improving the whole marketing team.

Be smart

You are the best person to judge which advice to follow and which to ignore. Companies have different policies and internal politics, and marketing teams have their own dynamics based on company size and the structure of the marketing department. You may want to slowly adapt your marketing meetings to follow the best practices presented here and may also decide to completely ignore a few. That's okay, as long as you get your own marketing meetings to be effective, then use what works for you.

Be persistent

Change is difficult, especially if it is perceived as requiring more work. The important thing is to not give up after the first try. Keep pushing and, even if it takes a while, you will be able to change the way marketing meetings are run. Don't give up and keep trying, after all, why have meetings unless they are effective?

Summary

Running marketing meetings is not as hard as you might initially think. It is all about identifying the correct meeting type, planning and preparing before the meeting, making sure you pay attention to some best practices for running meetings, and doing proper post-meeting follow-ups.

Although marketing meetings come in many forms, we covered the most typical types to help you understand that each one requires a different dynamic and will have different goals. For example, if you need to organize a planning meeting, you should focus on ending your meeting with a solid plan or clear next steps to get a marketing plan delivered. Alternatively, ending an evaluation and review meeting requires specific data points from the campaign to be discussed.

In some cases, the meeting type won't be discernible by its name or topic, so taking a look at the agenda will help you understand what type of meeting you are attending. If, on the other hand, you are the meeting organizer, making it clear the meeting goals will ensure all attendees can come prepared and with the right expectations.

With this in mind, planning and preparing for your meeting becomes easier and will ensure that you and your team can have a productive meeting. For that, we covered some best practices you can use either as the organizer or as a team member. These include setting clear goals, identifying the required attendees, and deciding on the meeting duration, place, equipment, and any advance preparation needed by the organizer and attendees.

Once your meeting is set up, conducting the meeting properly is more of an art than a science, but this shouldn't discourage you from trying different techniques when opening your meeting, getting everyone's input, and even trying out different technologies for brainstorming and note-taking.

Finally, we discussed some tips for following up after a meeting, which is typically what ensures that the meeting results will be disseminated, that agreed upon action items will be taken care of, and that your meeting was a good use of everyone's time.

If there's one thing I would like you to take away from this book, it is that although meetings, and marketing meetings in particular, can be challenging, by following the advice in this book, you can turn them into productive, fun sessions, and get you and your team to become more effective.

CPSIA information can be obtained at www.ICGtesting.com
Printed in the USA
BVOW01s1923191014

371291BV00003B/31/P

9 781783 000180